KU-213-408

# Families
## Relationships in art

by Ruth Thomson

HODDER
Wayland

An imprint of Hodder Headline Limited

**Titles in this series:**
Action!  Movement in art
Families: Relationships in art
Look At Me! Self-Portraits in art
Place and Space; Landscapes in art
Sculpture: Three dimensions in art
Telling Tales: Stories in art

For more information about this series
and other Hodder Wayland titles, go to
www.hodderwayland.co.uk

Series concept: Ruth Thomson
Series Consultant: Erika Langmuir
Editor and Picture Research: Margot Richardson
Designers: Rachel Hamdi and Holly Mann

Copyright © Ruth Thomson 2005

**British Library Cataloguing in Publication Data**
Thomson, Ruth
Family and friends: portraying relationships. - (Artventure)
1.Interpersonal relations in art - Juvenile literature
2.Art appreciation - Juvenile literature
I.Title
704.9'49302

ISBN 0 7502 45719

Printed in China

The publishers would like to thank the following for permission
to reproduce their pictures:
Page 1 Jan Steen, akg-images, London; 4-5 Wolverhampton Art
Gallery, West Midlands, UK/www.bridgeman.co.uk; 6-7 The
Walker, National Museums, Liverpool; 8 © David Hockney/
Tate, London 2004; 9 Alte Pinakothek, Munich, Germany,
Giraudon /Bridgeman Art Library/www.bridgeman.co.uk;
10  V&A Images, London; The work illustrated on page 11 has
been reproduced by permission of the Henry Moore
Foundation, from the Henry Moore Foundation Archive; 12 John
Ahearn/Alexander and Bonin, New York; 13 © Estate of Stanley
Spencer 2003, All Rights Reserved, DACS/© Leeds Museums
and Galleries (City Art Gallery) UK/www.bridgeman.co.uk; 14
© Christie's Images/CORBIS; 15 © Philadelphia Museum of
Art/CORBIS; 16 Burghley House Collection, Lincolnshire,
UK/www.bridgeman.co.uk; 17 Pierre-Auguste Renoir, akg-
images, London; 18-19 © Francis G. Mayer/CORBIS; 20 Louvre,
Paris, France, Giraudon/Bridgeman Art
Library/www.bridgeman.co.uk; 21 © Archivo Iconografico,
S.A./CORBIS; 22 © Succession H Matisse/DACS 2003/Photo ©
Board of Trustees, National Gallery of Art, Washington, from the
collection of Mr and Mrs Paul Mellon; 23 © Munch
Museum/Munch - Ellingsen Group, BONO, Oslo, DACS,
London 2003; 24-25 © Birmingham Museums and Art
Gallery,/www.bridgeman.co.uk; 26-27 Jan Steen, akg-images,
London.

**weblinks**

For more information about
families in art, go to
www.waylinks.co.uk/series/
artventure/families

# Contents

Words in **bold** can be found in the glossary

# Looking at families

Artists make images of families for many reasons. Some have painted **portraits** of their own families. Others have painted pictures of family groups specifically designed to impress, amuse or to give the viewer a message.

As you look at the works in this book, remember that the artists made deliberate choices about colours, the **setting**, grouping, and **poses** of the families they depicted. These all help to create a certain mood and show something particular about a family.

❏ Frederick Daniel Hardy
**Baby's Birthday**
*1867*

▲ See how many touches of red there are dotted all over the picture. These lead your eye to every important detail, and help to convey a feeling of glowing happiness.

A warm fire burns in the grate. ▲ Notice the jacket drying on the line above, the steaming kettle and the plate of toast warming on the fender.

## Country scenes

Frederick Daniel Hardy lived in an English village in the nineteenth century. Using local people as models, he painted **small-scale** country scenes, often of contented home life. He sold these to city dwellers, who liked to imagine that country people lived a more unspoiled and natural life than those who lived in crowded, filthy cities.

## A happy home

Hardy depicts this village family in a large, warm cottage. Look at how many tiny, realistic details about food, clothes, work and play the artist has included. Everyone is dressed in their best clothes for a party. The children are clean, plump and well-dressed. A fruit cake has been made for their tea. The eldest daughter has the privilege of lighting the candle on the cake. The mother has brought out her best tea set on a tray.

❏ Frederick Daniel Hardy
**Baby's Birthday (details)**

- What else are the family going to eat?
- What pets do the family have?
- How will the room be lit?
- What presents has grandmother brought?

## Father's work

The father has laid aside his tailor's needle, scissors and iron. An unfinished soldier's jacket lies on his table under the window, where there is most light. His card patterns hang on the wall and scraps of fabric litter the table.

## True country life?

In reality, country families were mostly poor and lived in cramped, damp cottages. Babies often died before their first birthday. Few children went to school. Instead, they worked in fields from dawn to dusk, six days a week. They were often underfed and rarely washed. Although Hardy's picture looks lifelike, it is not a true view of country life.

# A grand family

In the past, only very rich and important families could afford to have their portraits painted. They asked artists to paint an impressive image that portrayed the family as they wanted to be seen.

## Showing off

Sir Thomas Lucy lived in England during the seventeenth century. His family portrait shows off not only his wealth, **status** and many children, but also his special interests.

- What pet do the children have?
- Why is the woman in the cap behind the mother's chair, set apart from the rest of the family?
- Who do you think she might be?

The family is arranged in a room carpeted with an expensive **Oriental** rug, heavy velvet hangings and ornate chairs. Outside is a view of their extensive lands. The family are dressed in costly clothes and the mother is wearing her best jewellery.

⌐ Unknown artist (copy of painting by Cornelius Johnson, 1625) **Sir Thomas Lucy and Family**, *mid-18th century*

## The son and heir

Spencer, the eldest son, is shown apart from the main group, dressed in clothes similar to his father's. He is about to step into the house from the garden. This suggests his position as **heir**. When his father died, Spencer would inherit both the house and land, and become the new head of the family. The apples that he carries are a **symbol** of the growth and wealth that the family hope for in the future.

## Boys or girls?

Sir Thomas had seven children. It was the custom of the time for boys to wear skirts until the age of about six or seven. The girls wore a dress with a scooped neck, whereas the boys wore a skirt with a tight **bodice** like their father's. Look carefully at the picture to discover which of the children are girls and which are boys.

## Passions and pastimes

All sorts of clues reveal Sir Thomas's two particular **passions**. The dog with its large, alert eyes, behind Sir Thomas's chair, the hawk perching on a stool and the **spurs** on the table are all picture clues about his interest in hunting. The leather-bound books on the table represent Sir Thomas's library, of which he was extremely proud.

# Husband and wife

David Hockney, **Mr and Mrs Clark and Percy**, *1971*

These double portraits show two recently married couples.

## A fashionable couple
David Hockney, an English artist, painted this picture of well-known designers, Ossie Clark and Celia Birtwell. He was a great friend, and gave them the portrait as a wedding present.

Hockney set them in the living room of their smart, fashionable London house, with its modern table, chair and shaggy rug. There is no sense of closeness between the couple. Ossie, bare-footed, slumps in the chair with Percy, the cat, on his lap. Celia poses more formally, with her hand on her hip, wearing a dress that Ossie had designed for her.

□ Peter Paul Rubens
**Self-portrait with Isabella Brandt, his First Wife, in the Honeysuckle Bower**
*1609-10*

Compare the two pictures.
- What differences can you spot between them?
- What does this tell you about the people?

## The artist and his wife

Rubens, a **Flemish** artist, painted this portrait of himself and Isabella, his first wife, shortly after they married in 1609. Rubens was already a well-known painter and depicted himself as a wealthy, good-looking gentleman, dressed in a fine, elegant outfit. He has seated himself above his young wife, emphasizing his position both as her protector and master.

## A testament of love

The picture celebrates the joy of love and strength of marriage. The couple are shown in a garden, heavy with honeysuckle – both considered symbols of love. Rubens and Isabella lean together and **entwine**, just as honeysuckle does. Her hand rests on his, her skirt falls over his shoe and his hand seems to lie on her hat.

Trace your finger from Rubens' hat, around the outermost edge of his breeches, the bottom of Isabella's skirt and up along her arm and hat. These outlines form an oval. This is thought to be a symbol of **unity**, since it has no beginning or end.

9

# Babies

The first family relationship that most people have is with their mother, who cares for them when they are born. Throughout art in Europe, the mother and child has been a popular theme.

## Mary and Jesus

In the past, countless pictures and **sculptures** of Mary with Jesus as a child were made to decorate Christian churches. Antonio Rossellino, a fifteenth-century Italian sculptor, modelled this detailed image of them in **terracotta**. He shows Mary tilting her head towards this special child and protecting him with her arm, emphasizing her tenderness and devotion.

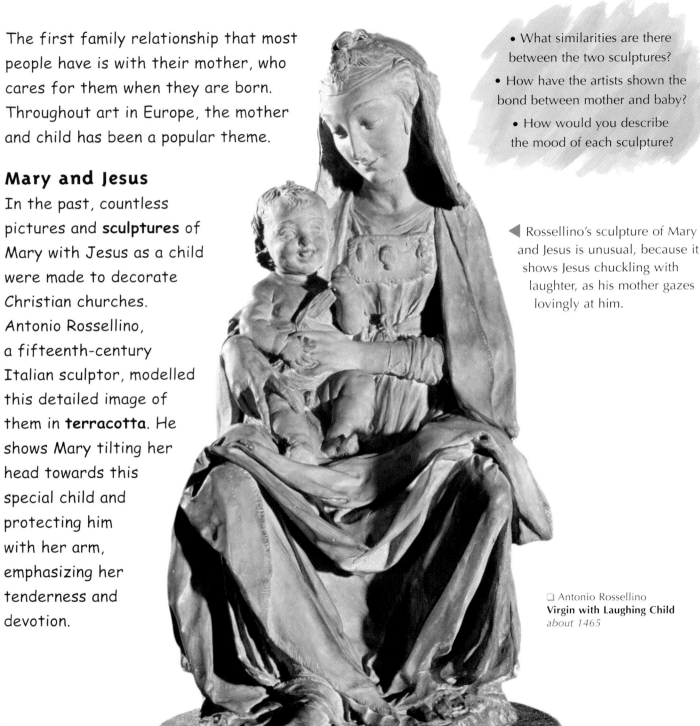

- What similarities are there between the two sculptures?
- How have the artists shown the bond between mother and baby?
- How would you describe the mood of each sculpture?

◀ Rossellino's sculpture of Mary and Jesus is unusual, because it shows Jesus chuckling with laughter, as his mother gazes lovingly at him.

❏ Antonio Rossellino
**Virgin with Laughing Child**
*about 1465*

Henry Moore was a twentieth-century English sculptor. When he became a parent himself, he became interested in the bond between mother and child.

## Rock-a-bye-baby

His bronze sculpture is full of shapes and angles that give it a sense of movement and playfulness. The mother seems to be rocking her chair as she swings her baby high in the air. The child looks as if it is kicking its legs in delight.

## Mother and child

Notice how Moore has simplified every detail of the mother. Her head is a strange shape. Her face has only tiny holes for eyes and no ears, nose or mouth. The length of her arms is exaggerated. Her skinny, **elongated** body and skirt double as the back and seat of the rocking chair. All these features add to the sense of movement. The child, by contrast, looks solid and more realistic.

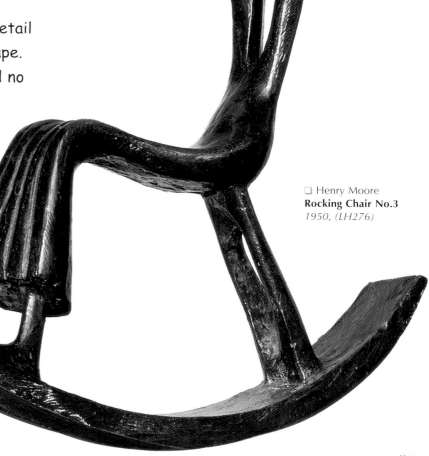

❏ Henry Moore
**Rocking Chair No.3**
*1950, (LH276)*

# Mothers

Body language can tell you a great deal about people's relationships. Compare these images of mothers and daughters.

## Perfect pleasure

This life-size sculpture is by John Ahearn, a contemporary American artist. It is cast from real people, and shows a daughter's whole-hearted love for her mother. The girl stretches up on tiptoes to give her mother a big hug. She presses against her mother to help keep her balance and throws back her head to gaze adoringly into her mother's eyes.

## Ill at ease

The mother, on the other hand, holds her body and arms stiffly. It's as if she were afraid that she might hurt herself if she gave her daughter a squeeze in return. With her thin body, blotchy skin and bandaged arm, she seems ill and fragile.

❑ John Ahearn
**Veronica and her Mother**
*1988*

□ Stanley Spencer
**Family Group: Hilda, Unity and Dolls**
*1937*

## A portrait of pain

The twentieth-century English painter, Stanley Spencer, divorced his first wife, Hilda. Soon after, he painted this portrait of her with Unity, their seven-year-old daughter.

## Divorce and dismay

Imagine the painter working on this picture. He knows that Hilda, feeling hurt and abandoned, would probably refuse to look at him. He shows her staring into the distance instead, deep in her own thoughts. She seems completely unaware of Unity, who, by contrast, fixes Spencer (and us, too) with a stern stare.

## Distressed dolls

Both Hilda and Unity hold dolls with empty eyes. The larger doll copies Unity's stare. The other, with **billowing** hair and a waving arm, seems to be thrashing about. Perhaps it is expressing Unity's hidden feelings?

# Fathers

Fathers have sometimes been portrayed with their eldest son – their heir.

## Paired portraits

These solemn portraits show a German prince and his six-year-old son; they lived in the sixteenth century. The boy is placed higher than his father, with more of his body revealed. This helps to show their difference in size.

## Close links

The two pictures are joined but the figures do not look towards each other. Instead, the painter has emphasized their family ties by repeating the two main colours. The black **background** of the boy's portrait matches his father's black coat and hat. The plain green background of the father's picture echoes his son's green hat and jacket.

❏ Lucas Cranach the Elder, **Portraits of Johann the Steadfast and his son Johann Friedrich the Magnanimous**, *1509*

## Like father, like son

Mary Cassatt, an American painting in the late 1800s, brings out the affection between a father and son in this fond portrait of her brother and her nephew.

Not only do they have similar hairstyles, eyes and expressions, but father and son both gaze in the same direction. Cassatt also welds their bodies together with a continuous band of black, making it impossible to tell where one ends and the other begins. Their relaxed pose suggest that they feel at ease with each other.

## Large and small

To show the contrast in size between adult and child, Cassatt has done the opposite of Cranach. She has **aligned** the two heads, but shown the boy, with his short legs, perched up on the arm of the chair.

❏ Mary Cassatt
**Portrait of Alexander J Cassatt and His Son, Robert Kelso Cassatt**
*1884-85*

• How have both artists used skin colour to contrast fathers and sons?

• How have they used background colours to bring out the figures?

• What decorations link father and son in Cranach's portraits?

15

# Brothers and sisters

These two pictures of brothers or sisters show them not only as individuals, but also express their family ties.

## Brotherly bonds

Isaac Oliver, a sixteenth-century English painter, was best known for his **miniature** portraits. In this portrait of the Browne brothers, each brother is clearly different in his size, face and hair. However, everything about their outfits is exactly the same – including their hats, shoes, sword belts and even the chains hanging around their necks.

## Brothers in arms

The close-knit feeling is reinforced by the way each brother holds or touches another, and also by the presence of the fourth man.

• Do you think the Browne brothers were rich or poor? How can you tell?

• What do the three sisters have in common?

In his contrasting pale outfit, the fourth ▼ man is marked as an outsider. He has taken off his hat as a sign of respect to the brothers.

❑ Isaac Oliver, **The Browne Brothers**, *1598*

## Three sisters

Renoir was a nineteenth-century painter. The three sisters he painted here are the daughters of his **patron**, Berard. It shows their interests and roles at different stages of childhood. Margot reads a book. Lucie holds a doll. Marthe is absorbed in the more grown-up task of sewing.

▲ Everything on the left of the picture, including Margot and her book, is painted in cool blues. On the right, the warm colours of the carpet on the table, the curtains and the flowers heighten the feeling of the sun streaming through the window. Hide each half in turn to compare them.

❏ Pierre-Auguste Renoir
**Children's Afternoon at Wargemont**
*1884*
Wargemont is the name of Berard's house near Dieppe, in northern France, where Renoir stayed for several summers.

# Three generations

Occasionally, artists paint portraits that show three **generations** of one family. Charles Willson Peale was an American painter who lived from 1741 to 1827.

Here, he shows his mother, wife, brothers, sisters, nurse and two children. He shows the cheerful warmth they feel for each other, and also highlights his roles as artist and teacher.

Charles, the artist, ▼ shows himself in front of an **easel,** holding a paint **palette**. He leans over his brothers who are sitting in front of him.

Margaret Jane, the artist's ▼ older sister, has one hand on Charles's shoulder and the other on his wife's shoulder, showing her closeness to both of them.

▼ Rachel, Peale's wife, sits in the centre holding baby Margaret. Peggy, the family's beloved nurse, stands behind, slightly apart from the family.

▼ Peale's mother sits bolt upright. His sister, Elizabeth, sitting next to her, was not originally in the picture, but was added much later.

⌐ Charles Willson Peale, **The Peale Family,** *about 1770–83 and 1808*

## Art in the family

Charles's two brothers are shown on the left of the painting. St. George is drawing a portrait of their mother. James, another brother, who later became a painter of miniatures, points a pencil at their mother, as if giving advice. Charles is leaning over them, as if also commenting on the drawing.

Charles sculpted the three **busts** on the mantlepiece: one is of his teacher, one is of his patron and the third is of himself.

## A long time in the making

Peale took more than thirty years to complete this painting. He began it near the beginning of his career, after he had been to England to study. When he decided to finish it, only two of the family were still alive. By this time, he had become one of America's best-known painters and had founded a museum.

- Who looks out towards you and who looks at other people in the family? Why might Peale have chosen to depict his family like this?
- How has Peale used people's hands to show affection in the family?
- How does Peale show his own skill at drawing?

❏ Charles Willson Peale, **The Peale Family**, (detail)

## Peale's signature

The curling peel is the artist's signature. It is a **pun** on his family name. Peale also included the fruit to show off his skill at painting **still life**, as well as portraits.

❏ Charles Willson Peale, **The Peale Family**, (detail)

## The family saviour

Argus, the dog, was an important part of the Peale family. When a fire broke out at their home, his loud barking woke them up and saved them from disaster.

# Family feelings

❏ Domenico Ghirlandaio, **An Old Man and a Boy**, *1490s*

## Loving looks

Ghirlandaio, an Italian, painted this portrait in the fifteenth century. It is probably of a man and his grandson, and is a tender, intimate portrayal of love. The pair gaze into each other's eyes, unaware of anything outside. The child rests his hand on the old man, whose red robe gives him a sense of stability and warmth. The child is not concerned that the old man is disfigured by his huge, warty nose. By contrast, the child, with his neat **profile** and thick, wavy, fair hair is the ideal of beauty for his time.

- How would you describe the child's expression?
- What clue tells you that the old man was wealthy?
- How does this portrait make you feel about the old man?

The French painter, Paul Gauguin, used intense **primary colours** and exaggerated poses to convey the unhappiness of the Schuffenecker family.

## Divided by colour

He divided the picture into two broad contrasting bands of blue and yellow. Schuffenecker's wife and her bored, listless children create a strong pyramid shape against the yellow floor.

She sits stiffly like a statue with a large clenched fist. Her red cheeks and stern expression reveal her anger. The father, Emile Schuffenecker, tiny, and dressed all in blue, stands in a blue corner, cut off from the rest of his family by his easel. His clasped hands, pleading eyes and hunched shoulders show he is trying to win over his wife. However, the children's vivid red coats act as a block between the parents, suggesting that there is disagreement between them.

# Life and death

❏ Henri Matisse
**Pianist and
Checker Players**
*1924*

Artists can create a mood of joy or grief in their paintings by their use of space, shapes, colour and **technique**.

## Calm and contentment

The living room of the French painter, Matisse, with its rich patterns and shades of brilliant red, vibrates with life.

The floor is tipped forward, bringing the comfortable room closer into our view. We are being invited to share this moment while the artist's children enjoy themselves, each deep in concentration. By including images of his paintings on the far wall, his violins and his empty armchair, Matisse suggests his own presence in the family.

## Sickness and sadness

The Norwegian painter, Edvard Munch, had a childhood of illness and loss. His mother died when he was five. His sister died when he was fourteen. He, too, was sickly and often unable to go to school.

## Pain and loss

Munch said, 'I paint not what I see, but what I saw.' In this picture of a deathly pale girl with her despairing mother, he relives his memories of family grief and suffering. Munch painted six versions of this picture and made many black and white versions as well.

❑ Edvard Munch
**The Sick Child**
*1907*

- How has Munch made the girl's head stand out?
- Compare the poses of the mother and the child. What feelings do they express?
- Why do you think Munch painted the mother without her face being visible?

## An awful atmosphere

There is no sense of space in this room. Munch wanted to make us feel as if we were there, sharing the sorrow and pain of the mother and her daughter. He deliberately painted the figures and objects in a blurry, scratchy way, using cold, shivery colours and thick layers of paint. These help to create an intense atmosphere of trembling and suffering.

# Family misfortune

In the nineteenth century, thousands of families, who could not make ends meet in Britain, left to live in other countries. This painting shows a family leaving by boat, not knowing what to expect, or if they will ever see their homeland again.

▼ These white cliffs at Dover are the last glimpse the ship's passengers have of England.

◀ The stormy sea suggests that the journey ahead may be difficult, both physically and mentally.

A sneering ▶ man shakes an angry fist at the country he has been forced to leave.

Brown ▶ used his daughter, Catty, as the model for this little girl.

◀ A tough sheet of heavy fabric protects the wife's knees from sea spray.

◻ Ford Madox Brown
**The Last of England**
*1852-55*

◀ A variety of cabbages hang around the boat – a means of keeping them fresh on the long voyage.

## A desperate departure

Ford Madox Brown was an English painter who lived from 1821 to 1893. This picture was inspired by the **emigration** of his sculptor friend, Thomas Woolner, and his family, who went to Australia in 1852. However, the artist used himself and his wife Emma as the actual models for the departing couple.

## In true light

The artist painted much of the picture in his back garden. He even posed his models outdoors in snowy weather. This was so he could capture the cold, leaden light on the scene, similar to that on a dull day at sea. The wisps of hair across the woman's face and the flying ribbon of her hat suggest the force of the wind.

## In sharp focus

Oval-shaped Christian religious paintings probably inspired Madox Brown to use the same shape. The curves focus your attention on the couple, just as they do in oval pictures of the Holy Family (Jesus, Mary and Joseph).

☐ Ford Madox Brown
**The Last of England (details)**

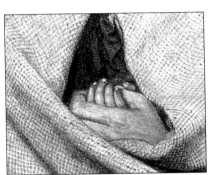

## Holding hands

Notice how the woman's gloved hand reveals an anxiety that her face doesn't show. She is squeezing her husband's oversized hand so hard, that the side of it has gone quite white.

Her other, bare hand grasps her baby's tiny hand. If you look closely at the main picture, you can see the shape of a tiny head bulging under the mother's cloak.

- How would you describe the man's expression?
- What do you think is on his mind?
- How would you describe the woman's expression?
- What are the other passengers on the boat doing?
- How has the man made sure that he won't lose his hat?

# A family celebration

❏ Jan Steen
**The Feast of
St. Nicholas**
*1663-65*

Jan Steen, a seventeenth-century Dutch artist, painted many amusing pictures of bustling, noisy families, which often showed people behaving badly. Parents at the time may have used these pictures to teach their children how to act well.

## A feast day

The family in this picture is celebrating the visit of St. Nicholas. According to Dutch **tradition**, St. Nicholas goes out, late at night on 5th December, delivering gifts to good children, which he puts in their shoes. In the morning, children wake up to find their treats. Notice the discarded shoe on the floor.

⊐ Jan Steen, **The Feast of St. Nicholas, (detail)**

The boy in the black hat behind her snivels because he found only a birch twig, the symbol of naughtiness, in his shoe. His older sister holds up the shoe while his younger brother points mockingly at it. Meanwhile, another brother (on the right) sings a song of thanks to St. Nicholas.

## Festive food

The basket of food in the foreground contains all sorts of traditional treats for St. Nicholas day: honey cake, gingerbread, apples, nuts and waffles.

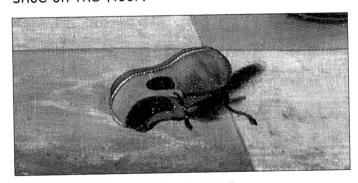

⊐ Jan Steen, **The Feast of St. Nicholas, (detail)**

The tallest, eldest boy points up the chimney, showing the baby how St. Nicholas came into the house. The little girl in the **foreground** clutches her new doll and has a bucket full of toys and sweets over her arm. She shies away from her mother, who puts out her hands, as if asking to see the doll.

⊐ Jan Steen, **The Feast of St. Nicholas, (detail)**

# About the artists

The symbols below show the size and shape of the works shown in this book, compared with an average-sized adult.

## John AHEARN (page 12)

(1951-) American
*Veronica and Her Mother*, 1988
Oil on fibreglass and wood, 180 x 90 x 90 cm
Alexander and Bonin, New York, USA

**Other family portraits**
❑ *Audrey and Janelle*, 1983
❑ *The Twins*, 2004
   Arizona State University, Tempe, Arizona, USA

## Ford Madox BROWN (pages 24-25)

(1821-1893) British
*The Last of England*, 1852-55
Oil on canvas, 82.5 x 75 cm
Birmingham Museums and Art Gallery,
Birmingham, UK

**Other family portraits**
❑ *Henry Fawcett: Millicent Fawcett*, 1872
   National Portait Gallery, London, UK

## Mary CASSATT (page 15)

(1845-1926) American
*Portrait of Alexander J. Cassatt and His Son, Robert Kelso Cassatt*, 1884-85
Oil on canvas, 100 x 81.2 cm
Philadelphia Museum of Art, Philadelphia, PA, USA

## Other family portraits
❑ *Young Mother*, 1900
   Metropolitan Museum of Art, New York, USA
❑ *The Child's Bath*, 1893
   The Art Institute of Chicago, Chicago, Illinois, USA

## Lucas CRANACH The Elder (page 14)

(1472-1553) German
*Portraits of Johann the Steadfast and his son Johann Friedrich the Magnanimous*, 1509
Oil on wood, left 41 x 31 cm; right 42 x 31 cm
National Gallery, London, UK

**Other family portraits**
❑ *Double Portrait of a Prince and Princess of Saxony*, about 1516-1518
   National Gallery of Art, Washington DC, USA
❑ *The Three Electors of Saxony*, about 1535
   Germanisches Nationalmuseum, Nuremburg, Germany

## Paul GAUGUIN (page 21)

(1848-1903) French
*The Schuffenecker Family*, 1889
Oil on canvas, 73 x 92 cm
Musée d'Orsay, Paris, France

## Domenico GHIRLANDAIO (page 20)

(c. 1449-1494) Italian (Florence)
*An Old Man and a Boy*, 1490s
Oil on panel, 62.7 x 46.3 cm
Louvre, Paris, France

**Other family portraits**
❑ *Madonna and Child*, 1470
   National Gallery of Art, Washington DC, USA
❑ *The Virgin and Child*,
   Louvre, Paris, France

## Frederick Daniel HARDY
(pages 4-5)

(1826–1911) English
*Baby's Birthday,* 1867
Oil on canvas, 66 x 91.4 cm
Wolverhampton Art Gallery, Wolverhampton, UK

**Other pictures of families**
❑ *The Chimney Sweep,* 1862
   Wolverhampton Art Gallery, Wolverhampton, UK
❑ *The Young Photographers,* 1862
   Tunbridge Wells Museum, Tunbridge Wells, UK

## David HOCKNEY (page 8)

(1937-) English
*Mr and Mrs Clark and Percy,* 1971
Acrylic on canvas, 213.4 x 304.8 cm
Tate Britain, London, UK

**Other double portraits**
❑ *My Parents,* 1977
   Tate Gallery, London, UK
❑ *American Collectors (Fred and Monica Wiseman),* 1968
   Art Institute of Chicago, Chicago, Illinois, USA

## Henri MATISSE (page 22)

(1869-1954) French
*Pianist and Checker Players,* 1924
Oil on canvas, 73.7 x 92.4 cm
National Gallery of Art, Washington DC, USA

**Other pictures of families**
❑ *The Painter's Family,* 1911
   Hermitage Museum, St Petersburg, Russia
❑ *The Music Lesson,* 1917
   Barnes Foundation, Lincoln University, Merion, PA, USA

## Henry MOORE (page 11)

(1898-1986) English
*Rocking Chair No.3,* 1952 (LH276)
Bronze, 32 cm high
Private Collection
Tate Britain, London, UK

**Other family sculptures**
❑ *Family Group,* 1946
   Museum of Modern Art,
   New York, USA
❑ *Family Group,* 1948-1949
   Tate Britain, London, UK

## Edvard MUNCH (page 23)

(1863–1944) Norwegian
*The Sick Child,* 1907
Oil on canvas, 120 x 118.5 cm
Nasjonalgalleriet, Oslo, Norway

**Other works**
❑ *Death in the Sickroom,* 1895
   Nasjonalgalleriet, Oslo, Norway
❑ *Death and the Child,* 1899
   Munch Museum, Oslo, Norway

## Isaac OLIVER (page 16)

(c. 1565-1617) English
*The Browne Brothers,* 1598
Gouache and watercolour on vellum on card,
24.1 x 26 cm
Burghley House Collection, Stamford,
Lincolnshire, UK

## Charles Willson PEALE (pages 18-19)

(1741-1827) American
*The Peale Family*
c.1770-83 and 1808
Oil on canvas, 143.5 x 227.3 cm
The New-York Historical Society, New York, USA

**Other family portraits**
❑ *The Staircase Group (portrait of Raphaelle Peale and Titian Ramsey Peale)*, 1795
Philadelphia Museum of Art, Philadelphia, PA, USA
❑ *Self-Portrait with Angelica and Portrait of Rachel*, c. 1782-85
The Museum of Fine Arts, Houston, Texas, USA

## Pierre-Auguste RENOIR (page 17)

(1841-1919) French
*Children's Afternoon at Wargemont*, 1884
Oil on canvas, 127 x 173 cm
Nationalgalerie, Berlin, Germany

**Other family portraits**
❑ *Madame Georges Charpentier and her Children*, 1878
The Metropolitan Museum of Art, New York, USA
❑ *The Daughters of Paul Durand-Ruel (Marie-Therese and Jeanne)*, 1882
The Chrysler Museum of Art, Norfolk, Virginia, USA

## Antonio ROSSELLINO (page 10)

(1427-1479) Italian
*Virgin with Laughing Child*, about 1465
Terracotta, 48.3 cm high
Victoria and Albert Museum, London, UK

**Other images of Mary and Jesus**
❑ *Madonna and Child*
Cleveland Museum of Art, Cleveland, Ohio, USA
❑ *Madonna and Child with Angels*, c. 1455-60
Metropolitan Museum of Art, New York, USA

## Peter Paul RUBENS (page 9)

(1577-1640) Flemish
*Self-Portrait with Isabella Brandt, his First Wife, in the Honeysuckle Bower*, 1609-10
Oil on canvas-covered panel, 178 x 136.5 cm
Alte Pinakothek, Munich, Germany

**Other family portraits**
❑ *Rubens, his Wife, Helena Fourment and their Son, Peter Paul*, c. 1639
The Metropolitan Museum of Art, New York, USA
❑ *Rubens and his Second Wife in their Garden*, 1630
Alte Pinakothek, Munich, Germany

## Stanley SPENCER (page 13)

(1891-1959) English
*Family Group: Hilda, Unity and Dolls*, 1937
Oil on canvas, 76.2 x 50.8 cm
Leeds Museums and Galleries (City Art Gallery), UK

## Jan STEEN (pages 26-27)

(1625/6-1679) Netherlands
*The Feast of St. Nicholas*, 1663-65
Oil on canvas, 82 x 70.5 cm
Rijksmuseum, Amsterdam, Holland

**Other family pictures**
❑ *Twelfth Night Feast*, 1662
Museum of Fine Arts, Boston, Mass, USA
❑ *The Lean Kitchen*, 1652-54
National Gallery of Art, Ottowa, Canada

## Unknown artist (pages 6-7)

British School
*Sir Thomas Lucy and Family*, mid-18th century
(Copy of painting by Cornelius Johnson, 1625)
Oil on canvas, 75 x 132 cm
Walker Art Gallery, Liverpool, UK

# Glossary

**Aligned** Placed in a straight line.

**Background** The part of a painting that appears to be furthest from the viewer.

**Billowing** Flowing outward in a wavy motion.

**Bodice** The part of a dress that fits tightly on the body above the waist.

**Bust** A sculpture of someone's head and shoulders.

**Easel** The stand on which artists rest a canvas for painting.

**Elongated** Made longer.

**Emigration** Leaving your own country to go and live for a long time in another country.

**Entwine** Wind or twist together.

**Flemish** From Flanders, a place that is now divided between Belgium, France and the Netherlands.

**Foreground** The part of a painting that seems closest to the viewer.

**Generation** A step in a family tree. You are a generation below your parents and they are a generation below your grandparents.

**Heir** The person who takes over the property and goods of a dead person.

**Miniature** A very tiny, detailed painting.

**Oriental** From the east, usually meaning the countries of South Asia.

**Palette** The wooden board on which artists lay out and mix their paints.

**Passion** Very intense liking for something or someone.

**Patron** Someone who asks and pays for an artist to make a specific work of art, or who supports artists by buying their work.

**Portrait** A painting, sculpture, photograph or drawing of a particular person.

**Poses** Particular positions where something or someone has been drawn, painted or photographed.

**Primary colours** Red, yellow and blue – pure colours that cannot be made by mixing any colours together.

**Profile** An outline of something, especially a face, seen from the side.

**Pun** A joke using the different meanings of a word, or words that sound the same.

**Setting** The surroundings or location of a place, or where an event happens.

**Small-scale** Small size or extent.

**Spurs** Sharp points that horse-riders sometimes wear on their heels. A rider kicks a horse with spurs to make it go faster.

**Status** High rank or social position.

**Still life** A picture of an arrangement of objects, such as flowers, food, utensils, tools or crockery.

**Symbol** Something that stands for something else.

**Technique** Way of carrying out a particular task, especially of an artistic work.

**Terracotta** Brown clay used for making pottery and sculpture and then fired in a very hot oven, called a kiln, to make it hard.

**Tradition** Customs or beliefs that are passed on from parents to children.

**Unity** Being united or forming a whole.

# Index

Numbers in **bold** show page numbers of illustrations